GRAB

AND

HOLD

THEIR

ATTENTION

By Paul Scelsi

Why read Paul Scelsi's book about improving your presentations?

Here's what audiences have said after attending HIS presentations...

"Paul is one of the most dynamic speakers I have encountered throughout my adult career...how he uses both verbal and body language to emphasize key points. It is remarkable to watch as he captures the audience's attention and keeps them engaged." – **Sean Van Dyke, Franciscus Incorporated**

"Paul is one of the best public speakers I've seen in the business world. His passion and preparation make him very effective delivering a message that is not an easy one for people to get excited about (attic ventilation). He has a gift for making it bigger than it might otherwise be." – **Chuck Jerasa, former Group President Building Products, Gibraltar Industries**

"Paul is enthusiastic, energetic and engaging. To make the topic of attic ventilation interesting is a feat in itself." – **Chris Arrington, Arrington Roofing**

"Paul has a gift in his ability to connect with his audience. No matter the content, he is able to capture the audience's attention in the first few seconds. He reminds me of a boxer that is anxiously awaiting the bell to ring; once he hears that bell, he is moving around the room and hitting you from all angles. His voice modulations might be what separates him from the rest. Fantastic public speaker." – **Brian Haislip, former Lowe's National Account Manager, Gibraltar Industries**

"I think the world of Paul's presentation skills. I have invited him to be a guest speaker for our ASHI chapter because of the information he provides and his ability to deliver a great presentation that is captivating." – **Brian "B.K." Thompson, King Home Inspection, LLC**

"Paul has amazing energy! He brings the best information, experience and knowledge to teach and motivate. A must-see for anyone in the roofing or ventilation industry." – **Sue McCollum May, A Better Way Construction & Roofing, LLC**

"Paul promises an informative, fast-paced presentation on the principles of attic ventilation inside an attic cavity and he absolutely crushes it. He has taken the seminar across the nation and it has become a yearly event that our company looks forward to." – **Jeff Barnett, Barnett Roofing and Siding, Inc**

Author Bio

Since 1998, Paul Scelsi has been a public speaker and seminar host in the residential roofing building materials industry across North America. He has written dozens of articles for trade publications and his work appears in YouTube videos. He has a bachelor's degree in communications from Temple University, Philadelphia, Pennsylvania. He's an avid runner who met his wife while training for the Dallas Marathon. He lives in Plano, Texas with his wife Holli, their daughter Stella and dog Lily. This is his first book.

Dedication

Dedicated to my wife Holli and daughter Stella for encouraging me along the way and tolerating my many presentation rehearsals throughout the house. Special appreciation for my Dad, Mom, brother Sal, and sisters Gloria and Chris.

Contents

Acknowledgements

In 8th grade at Our Lady of Calvary Elementary School in northeast Philadelphia, I delivered a campaign speech to the 6th, 7th and fellow 8th graders as I ran for Treasurer in our school's launch of a Student Council. Shortly after, my English Literature teacher, **Mrs. McIntyre,** asked me to consider representing our school in speech competitions against other area schools. She recommended Martin Luther King's "I Have a Dream" speech for me. Her belief in me sparked something that burns inside me to this day – a deep desire to create and present messages.

At Archbishop Ryan High School in northeast Philadelphia, Media teacher, **Mr. Clothier,** thought the school newspaper's sports editor (me) would be interested in hosting a show on the school's closed-circuit TV station WARB featuring Ryan's various sports teams. I was more than interested. "Sports Shorts" live and sometimes prerecorded continued to fuel my interest in public speaking. Those years on camera in front of the student body still hold a special place in my heart decades later. I cherished my time in the TV studio with Mr. C and picked up many valuable communication tips.

My parents **Salvatore** and **Gloria Scelsi** worked tirelessly and made significant personal sacrifices to raise 4 children who together are barely 4 years apart in age oldest to youngest: my brother Sal, sisters Gloria and Chris, and me. The example was set at a very young age to set goals, work hard to achieve them and take pride in your work. It took me becoming a parent myself to fully understand and appreciate what my parents provided. I think my father would be proud of this book and my mother, of course, is my biggest fan. Thank you, Dad and Mom.

I want to thank my brother **Sal Scelsi** and sister **Chris Scelsi** for their constant words of encouragement and suggestions as I wrote this book. Sal put me in touch with author **Mark Kram** who provided essential guidance throughout.

When I started public speaking and managing my employer's seminar program, I telephoned my oldest sister **Gloria Salvi** in a panic. I was feeling overwhelmed realizing I would be both the host of the entire program and the speaker. All across North America. How could I properly handle all of it? Gloria calmed me down with very basic yet practical sisterly advice I use to this day: Make a comprehensive master list of every necessary action step, arrange the steps in a timing sequence, and then tackle them one-by-one gaining confidence as I progressed. I miss you, Gloria.

So many people in my life lent helping hands toward the writing of this book. My in-laws **Judi** and **Larry Pilgrim** were instrumental in identifying chapters to include and offered suggestions to the overall flow of the text. My employer **Air Vent Inc.** gave me the awesome opportunity to be a public speaker hosting their seminars. Thank you, **Sam Ansley**! Over the years I had the special privilege to co-present seminars across North America with **Jeff Hansen**, **Mike Daniels**, **Kurt Mankell**, **Chuck Avola**, **Dustin Ciepliski**, and **Phil Grisham**. Aside from the memories we made as travel companions away from our families, you also provided tips and advice specific to public speaking and audience interaction that I use to this day. Thank you to the many seminar attendees over the years who praised me in person or via the feedback form for being a dynamic presenter. Your comments continue to motivate me.

People sometimes need sparks in their lives to act, to pursue a goal, to make things happen. This book needed a spark. Despite being on my "wish list" of goals for nearly 10 years, it took the repeated encouragement and follow-up of a former coworker, **Octavian Avila**, to get it started. Another coworker, **Jennifer Anderson**, probably thought her positive comments about my public speaking skills were insignificant. Hardly that, her words combined with Octavian's further powered me to start writing. Thank you, both.

Once I started writing the book, many **family members**, **friends**, **business associates** and **coworkers** allowed me to share my excitement and progress with them. Too kind to tell me I was bombarding them, they patiently and graciously provided encouragement and support. Thank you, all of you. Knowing I will not remember everyone, I nevertheless want to thank **Danielle Dunn, Ginny Walter, Phillip John, Shelly Doubet, Keana Booker, Brian Haislip, Jackie Phillips, Elizabet Salinas, Corrine Ondush** and **Joe Kanefsky**. I will forever be grateful.

To all of my **Air Vent** coworkers past and present as well as the Air Vent Sales Representatives I have worked with across North America, thank you. You have helped me more than you realize.

A few hours before I would take the stage for an important presentation at the **Air Vent** Leadership Meeting, my wife, **Holli Scelsi,** sent me a text message that included this quotation from Oprah Winfrey: *"Know what sparks the light in you. Then use that light to illuminate the world."* I loved it. It made me smile and excited me for the upcoming presentation even more. That's what my wife has been for me from the start – an encouraging source of motivation, drive and excitement. Thank you, Holli, for keeping our family afloat all the many years I am on the road public speaking and for all that you do to make our house a home for me, our daughter Stella and Lily our cute Maltese.

Just days before I sat down to start writing this book, I told my wife **Holli** and then 9-year-old daughter **Stella Scelsi** that I am finally going to start. I'm finally going to stop talking about the book and start to write it. Stella said, "Will the book you write be on the shelves at Barnes & Noble, Daddy?" Well...

Introduction

I believe the primary goal of a presenter (whether through a speech, video, business meeting, seminar, etc.) is to understand the message internally that ultimately needs to be delivered to a target audience in a compelling, easy-to-understand and memorable manner. And if taking action (whatever that "action" is) is one of the results intended for the audience, that is much more likely to happen if the delivered message is compelling, easy to understand and memorable.

Since 1998, I have had the privilege to present an educational seminar to residential roofing professionals across North America about the benefits of proper attic ventilation. ATTIC VENTILATION. Doesn't that sound exciting? I know it doesn't. The target audience doesn't always find it particularly interesting on the surface; and if anyone should, it's them!

Thankfully, I have been able to transform a mundane topic into a powerful presentation that informs, engages and motivates the audience into action. You can, too. Regardless of the topic. This book will show you how.

May the messages we create and deliver – Stand Out.
Be Memorable. Cause Action.

Section One:

Backstage Prep

SECTION 1, CHAPTER 1

Put Yourself in YOUR Audience

"The success of your presentation will be judged not by the knowledge you send but by what the listener receives."
– Lilly Waters

The best advice I can give someone who wants to improve the way they *create* and then *present* a speech, a video, a business meeting, a seminar or any type of presentation is this: <u>Imagine you are actually in *YOUR OWN* audience.</u> Before you begin creating content and practicing the delivery of that content, pretend you are literally in one of the seats in your audience about to sit through *YOUR* talk. What would quickly grab *your* attention? And what would keep *your* attention for the duration? What key information do *you* expect to walk away with when the presentation is over? How would you want that information delivered (presented, explained) to *you*?

Answering these questions requires having a solid understanding of your audience's expectations. Thus, you have to do some homework on the front end. This checklist of audience expectations I ask myself before creating content has helped me.

- o **What is the overall purpose of the presentation?** In other words, if I were an attendee of this presentation, what will I take home with me? And why is it important that I go home with this information? I try to answer these questions in a few short sentences.

- o **What topics or main points will support the overall purpose of the presentation?** I list them. They become the main sections within the overall presentation.

- o **What words, facts, examples, stories, statistics, quotations, etc. would I want or expect to hear during the presentation?** I make a list of everything I believe is essential to help me explain the message. And I start researching the various elements I can find to insert into the presentation.

Let's say, for example, you've been invited to make a presentation to a group of marketing managers about the importance of using social media in your day-to-day marketing programs. I recommend early in the content creation process that you imagine you are the marketing manager in attendance who is hopeful to learn why social media is important and how to use social media. Make a list of the questions you would have as the marketing manager in attendance. For each question you ask, find the answer and incorporate those answers into the content of your presentation.

Likewise, step into the shoes of your audience and give serious thought to how they would expect or want to have the information delivered to them. Should the pace be slow or fast or a combination of both? Should you involve the audience during the delivery or keep it a one-way flow of information; presenter to audience? To help you ask and answer these questions I will share with you throughout the book what has worked very successfully for me. It can work well for you, too, I believe.

Are you ready to grab their attention?

SECTION 1, CHAPTER 2

Grab their Attention Immediately

"The beginning is the most important part of the work." – **Plato**

We have one chance to capture the audience's attention
<u>immediately</u>. That's at the start of our presentation (or video,
speech, business meeting, seminar, etc.). Give extra attention
to the words you will use and how you will speak those words
so that the listener's attention will be grabbed right way. You
might be wondering, "What's the big deal with capturing
their attention right out of the gate? Why can't I grab their
attention a few minutes into the presentation after the
audience warms up to me?" Because it may be too late by
then. In my experience, the audience is at its most invested
attention at the very start. Generally speaking, the audience's
focus, energy and willingness to listen is at its peak at the
start. They are ready to listen and give you their full
attention. Every minute that passes after the very opening
comments is a chance for their attention to slip away. We're
not going to let it slip away. We're going to seize full control
of their attention at the very beginning and – if you follow
the principles outlined throughout this book – never let it go
until the end.

How do we grab their attention immediately? With <u>boldly written</u> and <u>powerfully delivered</u> words. Here are two examples of opening comments I would make to an audience.

> (If I were delivering a presentation to beginning runners about **"Running Can Change Your Life for the Better"**)

> ***"I am living proof that running can change your life for the better. I'm going to tell you how right now."***
> From there the presentation continues...

> (If I were delivering a presentation to managers about **"The Power of Saying 'Thank You' to Employees"**)

> ***"You want your employees to be self-driven to produce high quality work? Start thanking them for their past work. When you praise someone and genuinely thank someone, they'll continue to deliver results worthy of even more praise and gratitude."***

If you commit to working on this during the writing (creation) of your presentation and well into your rehearsals (delivery) of your presentation, you will become a presenter who grabs your audience's attention.

Now let's keep their attention.

Hold their Attention Throughout

"Know what sparks the light in you. Then use that light to illuminate the world."
– Oprah Winfrey

Once you have hold of your audience's attention, never let go. Hold their attention until the very end. Some of the most personally special praise I have received from audiences is, "You made a rather dull topic interesting" and "I was so engaged in the presentation that time elapsed so quickly." The essence of both of those compliments is I was able to keep the audience's attention from start to finish and they were fully invested in the moment. That does not happen by accident. It takes a focused effort and commitment to your craft.

Sprinkled throughout this book are strategies that have worked well for me both in creating content (see Section Two on page 17) and in delivering that content (see Section Three on page 40) in a manner that keeps the audience alert, engaged and interested the entire time.

It begins with starting a conversation.

SECTION 1, CHAPTER 4

Keep it Conversational

"Think like a wise man but communicate in the language of the people."
– William Butler Yeats

To maximize the opportunity for your message to be warmly received and understood by your audience, I recommend you approach your overall presentation (or speech, video, business meeting, seminar, etc.) with the mindset: *I'm about to have a conversation with my audience* (NOTE: This applies even if your audience never has an opportunity to talk to you during the presentation.). You're not lecturing the audience. Instead, you're delivering your message in a conversational, friendly and engaging manner – both in the way you <u>choose the words</u> you are saying and in the way you <u>speak those words</u>. Regardless how technical the subject matter is, be conversational. You can have a conversation about a technical topic. You can have a conversation about anything, in fact.

If you can manage to always think of your presentation as an extended conversation (possibly with dozens or hundreds of people simultaneously), you'll **write it** and then **speak it** in a very warm, inviting and easy-to-understand manner. To help you write and present in a conversational manner, I have included chapters in this book about eye contact (see "Make Eye Contact" on page 51), using strategic pauses (see "Pause...to Pull Them In" on page 56), varying your volume (see "Vary Your Volume" on page 58), and incorporating transitions that connect one thought or topic to the next just like a flowing conversation (see "Use Transitions to Maintain Flow and Engagement" on page 12).

You can use your rehearsal time (see "Practice Often" on page 41) to double-check if in fact you have written your presentation in a conversational style. As you speak aloud your presentation based on the notes you have written, the conversational elements should flow naturally. If they do not, make adjustments and fine-tune the content.

That fine-tuning should include *incorporating transitions between sections to help keep your audience hooked – and that's our next topic.*

Use Transitions to Maintain Flow and Engagement

"Good transitions can make a speech more important to the audience because they feel they are being taken to a positive conclusion without having to travel a bumpy road." – **Joe Griffith**

We are story tellers. A strong presentation is a strong "story." A well-written and delivered story draws the audience in from the start and keeps the audience hooked throughout. Transitions between topics/sections within the "story" (presentation, video, speech, business meeting, etc.) help achieve this. It also keeps the entire presentation flowing smoothly; smoothly like a conversation (see "Keep it Conversational" on page 10).

As I create and eventually deliver a presentation, I make a conscious effort to connect one section to the next to help the audience follow along on the road we are traveling together. It's also an effective way to briefly summarize the previous point before moving onto the next point. Furthermore, transitions give the listener a mental break or pause: "OK. We're finished with topic ABC. Now let's see what XYZ is all about next."

Here are a few examples of how I try to incorporate strategic transitions between topics:

> *"Now that we understand how most adults use social media to learn about a brand or product, let's explore how a marketing manager can tap into social media to increase product and brand awareness."* (For example, if I were delivering a presentation about **"Using Social Media in Marketing"**).

> *"If you commit to gradually increasing your mileage as little as a quarter of a mile every other run, you'll eventually cover more and more miles. Your base foundation of mileage will build. Once you have a solid base of mileage, you can begin to work on your speed. Here's how."* (For example, if I were delivering a presentation about **"Starting a Running Program as a Form of Fun and Fitness"**).

Now it's time for the powerful one-two punch: content and passion.

SECTION 1, CHAPTER 6

Combine Content *and* Passion

"Effective communication is 20% what you know and 80% how you feel about what you know." – **Jim Rohn**

Not every subject or topic is inherently interesting; at least not on the surface at first glance. It's been my experience even the very people who are employed in the industry of the subject matter do not automatically find it interesting (residential attic ventilation, for example). Some may. But for many it's part of a "job they do that helps to pay the bills." It plays a functional role. It does not have built-in interest or excitement.

That's where a good presenter comes into play. It's the presenter's responsibility to bring interest and excitement to the topic through the <u>content creation process</u> and the <u>delivery/presenting of that content</u>. And that's the essence of the remainder of this book and its two next sections.

If you the presenter (or person delivering the speech or the person in the video, etc.) are not excited about the subject matter, how can you expect the audience to be excited about it and willing to engage with you? Again, not every topic or subject matter automatically carries with it built-in excitement and interest. If your topic is, "How to win a million dollars" or "Three easy steps to a FREE vacation," they carry some built-in excitement. The audience generally will be interested and fairly excited. But what if your topic is, "The best way to ventilate the attic of a house"? As the presenter, you're going to have to generate the excitement.

I believe strongly that the best presenters combine meaning-ful, useful content and deliver that content passionately in a compelling and memorable manner. It's not enough to just have good content. And it's not enough to just have passion. As presenters, we must combine the two. Good content presented in a dull, mundane manner will not stick with the audience long-term. Likewise, a passionately delivered presentation of weak, irrelevant material will not endure long-term. But combined, quality content and passion are the winning ingredients of top presentations. I urge you to be contagiously excited and energetic about the useful, relevant content you create.

Ready to create content?

Section Two

Creating Useful, Memorable Content

I enjoy writing and creating content. But I *love* presenting. There's something extra thrilling and exciting about being on "stage" in front of an audience and delivering a message to them. This includes videos, business meetings, speeches, seminars, etc. However, there is no presentation to stand on "stage" and deliver if someone has not taken the necessary time to write and create the content. Writing and creating builds the foundation so you can eventually deliver the presentation. And while it's the less glamorous part of the overall presentation process, it's just as important. Please give writing and creating your full effort and commitment. It'll pay big dividends in the end. We focus on that in this section.

Identify the Primary Purpose

"If you don't know what you want to achieve in your presentation your audience never will." – **Harvey Diamond**

An essential first step when creating the content of a presentation, video or seminar is to step back for a minute and ask yourself: **What is the primary purpose of the message?** What one key point do I hope to convey to the listener? You may be thinking as you read this, "There are multiple points I plan to communicate to the audience, not just one." I challenge you to dig deep to identify one **_PRIMARY_** point because that primary point will drive the presentation's clarity of content start to finish. It will force you to simplify a clear message you plan to write (and ultimately deliver). Yes, there will be sub-points you will bring to the table during the presentation, but they are not the primary topic. They are supporting ideas assisting the understanding of the primary point. Here's an example.

One of my passions is outdoor running. I met my wife running and I enjoy many benefits through participating in the sport. Let's say I wanted to share my joy of running with others and I was invited by a local running specialty store to give a talk to adults who were curious about the sport but have zero experience with it. This is how I would begin to write that presentation:

> **Step 1:** I would ask myself: What one point do I want to communicate to the listener? What is the one primary point I want to deliver?

> It would be this: "**Running Can Change Your Life for the Better: Here's How and How to Get Started.**"

From that starting point I would then begin to list the supporting elements that explain specifically how running can change your life for the better and how someone can start running. Those supporting elements or sub-topics become the various sections of the overall presentation (or speech or video or seminar).

Let's take a look at supporting topics next.

List the Supporting Topics

"When speaking in public, your message – no matter how important – will not be effective or memorable if you don't have a clear structure." – **Patricia Fripp**

In the previous chapter we identified the primary purpose of an example presentation I am creating. It is – **"Running Can Change Your Life for the Better: Here's How and How to Get Started."** Now it's time to list all of the topics that support the primary purpose. They will assist the understanding of the primary theme. They will become the sections of the presentation. I'll worry about their sequence another time. For now, I'll just list all of the supporting topics.

This is how I would begin to list all of the supporting topics:

Step 2: I would put myself in my own audience pretending I am listening to my own presentation (or video or seminar) and ask myself, "What would I want to hear and see to convince me that running does indeed change my life for the better AND what would

help me start running?" Then I would begin my list.
Here's what a partial list might look like.

1. Running improves my health.
2. Running puts me in a better mood.
3. Running energizes me.
4. Running helps me relieve stress.
5. Running allows me to enjoy Mother Nature (when I run outdoors).
6. Running gives me "ME" time (when I run alone).
7. Running gives me social time with friends and family (when I run with others).
8. Running can introduce me to new relationships (I met my wife while participating in a group running program at Run On for the Dallas Marathon).
9. Running gives me time to think through any work and family situations that are on my mind (i.e. challenging work projects, unexpected house repairs, etc.).
10. Running keeps me feeling young.

Continuing to build my list of topics, I would transition to the portion of the presentation focused on "How to get started running." Here's a partial list.

1. Set modest beginning goals to avoid disappointment/frustration (i.e. "Today I'll run ½ block and walk ½ a block.").

2. Pick a time of day I am most likely to stick with. (That's early morning before going to work for me).

3. Get sized and fitted for appropriate running shoes that fit my foot and accommodate how I land each stride. (I recommend a local running specialty store).

4. Buy moisture-wicking shorts and shirts (Avoid cotton).

5. Start a journal to document my progress (In time, it will be a source of pride and motivation looking back how far I've come).

6. Gradually increase mileage.

7. Work on speed.

8. Find someone to run with if it helps me stay committed.

9. Sign up for a local race to give me a goal to look forward to.

10. Save my race bibs inside a binder as a special keepsake. (I have the bib from every race I have ever run with hand-written notes of what was special about the race that day. They bring back many fond memories in my life.).

Once the list of supporting topics is complete, it's time to go back and insert content that drives home each point to help the audience understand and hopefully believe the message.

Let's enhance the message now.

Enhance the Content

"You are not being judged. The value of what you are bringing to the audience is being judged." – **Seth Godin**

In the previous chapter we listed the various supporting topics that point to the primary purpose of the presentation. Now it's time to add any content that will help make each supporting topic easy to understand, believable and – if we're effective – motivate the audience into action. I call this the meat and potatoes of the presentation. You've declared your primary purpose. You're unveiling your supporting topics along the way. And now you're driving home each point with substance.

Here's where that substance could come from:

> **Step 3:** What <u>specific details</u> will the audience require (Ask yourself: "What would *I* require if *I* were in my own audience?") to fully understand, believe and feel motivated to take action specific to each supporting point? It's been my experience that

audiences best receive and act on my messages when I have sprinkled into the presentation the following:

- o Statistics/data
- o Testimonials
- o Personal examples
- o Research/test results
- o Information from appropriate publications and experts in the specific field

Any content you can find that will help you communicate the supporting point is a candidate for inclusion here. I tend to err on the side of collecting too much substance during the creating process knowing that I can always delete. I'd rather have too much and not need it all, than be struggling to write a well-rounded presentation that may not impact the audience.

On page 19 we identified a potential presentation theme or primary purpose: **"Running Can Change Your Life for the Better: Here's How and How to Get Started."** We then listed 10 supporting topics specific to *"HOW running can change your life"* (page 21) as well as 10 supporting topics specific to *"HOW to get started"* (page 22). To add substance to these supporting topics, go down the list – one-by-one – inserting whenever possible relevant, impactful statistics, testimonials, personal examples, as well as information you can gather from research, appropriate publications, and experts in the specific field. That process adds meat and potatoes to your presentation. That's what will help your audience understand, believe and act on your message.

Here are two examples of adding substance to supporting topics.

> For the supporting topic **"Running improves my health"** (page 21), I'll insert documented research I can find that shows that regular exercise such as running helps to:
>
> a. Manage my weight (helping me to avoid problematic weight gain)
> b. Keep my blood pressure at a healthy level
> c. Reduce my risk of a heart attack
> d. Etc.
>
> For the supporting topic **"Set modest beginning goals to avoid disappointment/frustration"** (page 22), I'll provide examples of modest goals that are highly possible for the beginner runner:

a. Tell yourself, today I will run 20 yards and walk 20 yards and I'll repeat it 3 times.

b. Aim for doing it 3 times the first week (Monday, Wednesday and Saturday, for example).

c. Commit to it for at least 4 weeks before entertaining thoughts of quitting. Give it some time to show you, "This is indeed a very worthwhile activity for me."

d. Etc.

Continue this approach for all remaining <u>supporting topics</u> and the <u>substance</u> you want to give each topic. When you're finished writing a first draft, read it over start-to-finish with a focus on:

o Is it easy to understand?

o Would I believe it if I were in the audience listening to it?

o Is it thorough enough for me to start practicing how to present it?

When you can answer "yes" to all three questions above, you're ready to transition into rehearsal mode (see "Practice Often" on page 41).

BONUS Content Creation TIP:

I recommend you develop an eye for always being on the "lookout" for content in your daily reading and viewing of the content you regularly consume. I am always looking for possible content for my presentations. I keep files containing possible content ideas that I come across throughout the year {newspaper articles, clever advertisements inside magazines, catchy headlines I come across, etc.}. I may never use the content ideas that I collect. But I may.

We'll look at the advantages of having an inventory of ideas in the next chapter.

Collect More Notes than You'll Use

"Only the prepared speaker deserves to be confident." – **Dale Carnegie**

A presentation that I regularly deliver in the residential building materials industry lasts 2 hours. But my speaker's notes for that presentation have enough content for 4+ hours. Why so much extra content? For a number of reasons.

a) As I have added new content to the presentation over the years, I keep the old content in the notes just in case I one day decide to bring it back. I'll have it handy. It will not be a major chore to get my hands on historical content.

b) If I get stumped by an audience member's question about a topic that used to be included in my presentation that I used to know very well but no longer is featured in the program, I can revisit the subject easy enough after the presentation so I don't get stumped the next time. My comprehensive notes will make the information available at my fingertips.

c) If I anticipate tomorrow's audience is likely going to ask a question about content that I used to deliver but have since phased out, I can easily brush up on that subject area in the days leading up to the presentation. Again, it will not be a major investigative task to track down the historical content because it's already in my notes.

d) I use my speaker's notes as the foundation for the **current** presentation but also as a library of content for <u>tomorrow, next year and far into the future</u>. Maybe it's the schooled journalist in me, but I am always evaluating what I see and hear daily in my life with the mindset, "Would this fit in the presentation?" All it takes is a "maybe" and it goes into my speaker's notes. I may never use the information. But I just might. And I like having it handy and ready to use.

When it's time to select the notes that will be used in delivering the actual presentation (speech, video, seminar, etc.), they still often end up being much longer in length than what I end up presenting. That's because I continue to fine-tune during rehearsals and even after live presentations if I determine adjustments are needed. It's an ongoing process that begins with always being on the lookout for content.

I encourage you to build a large base of speaker's notes. You'll find value in their comprehensiveness and easy access (I "keyword search" my notes in Microsoft Word to find what I'm looking for) anytime you want to rehearse, fine-tune and re-visit your presentation's content.

I have found a wealth of potential presentation content by regularly reading; which we'll discuss next.

SECTION 2, CHAPTER 11

Read to Stay Current and Creative

"Grasp the subject, the words will follow."
– Cato the Elder

I have found that a great source of my presentation content can be found by staying on top of my industry or subject matter through reading regularly – magazines, newspapers, books, etc. whether they are digital or paper-based. Being current on my subject matter not only keeps me relevant to my target audience, it paves an easier path to replacing older content I'm starting to think is getting stale. Additionally, by staying current with my industry, I have conversation material I can bring up before, after or during breaks within the presentation.

Read as often as you can. I have always enjoyed reading so it's not too challenging for me to carve out time to read about my chosen subject matter. But if you do find it hard to regularly read, here are two suggestions:

- Designate a time of day to read for 15-20 minutes. Make it part of your daily routine. If you skip a day or two, it's OK. Just try to aim for reading most days.

- As you read and find material that might be useful in your presentation, highlight the sections of importance and place them in a folder. It will motivate you to keep reading (and finding possible future presentation content) as you see your folder expand. *And that will boost your confidence as you start to build your slideshow; which is what we discuss next.*

Use a Slideshow to Enhance Your Presentation

"Creativity is intelligence having fun."
– Albert Einstein

A well written/created slideshow can be a powerful enhancement to your presentation. Notice I used the word "enhancement." The slideshow <u>is not</u> the presentation. It's a tool to help the overall presentation. The actual presentation is a combination of the spoken words of the presenter, the presenter's body language and passion, audio and visual aids, and any audience handouts. I emphasize this because it's important to not lean on the slideshow as a crutch for the presentation. Count on the slideshow as a detailed outline that will help you deliver the message to the audience. But it's not the whole message. I discuss this in greater detail in "Do Not Read Your Slideshow to the Audience," on page 66. Here are my suggestions for creating a slideshow that is useful for **both the presenter and the audience**.

- Think of the slideshow as your detailed outline of topics. Let that guide you as you create it. Allow the bulleted items in your slideshow to both help trigger more discussion points from you while simultaneously allowing your audience to thoughtfully follow along.

- Write the bullets in as few words as possible to minimize how much your audience has to **read**. Remember, you can **speak** aloud all the words you want about the bulleted item.

- Showcase particularly compelling statistics, facts, quotations, etc. I like to call these "Wow" moments. Display them boldly on screen in your slideshow. This will draw extra attention to them.

- Incorporate photographs, short video clips, graphics, charts, etc. for anything that may be particularly complicated to explain or for your audience to understand. A combination of well-thought-out spoken words by the presenter with descriptive visuals (either during or after) can get the point across well.

- Do not give the audience your slideshow. Keep it as an exclusive element of your overall presentation that is only experienced by the live audience. You can certainly pass out handouts that may include portions of the slideshow, but I would think twice before releasing the actual slideshow itself. Some in your audience may object to this approach. That's OK. Audience objections come with the territory.

You'll be ready for audience objections because you'll plan for them as we discuss in the next chapter.

Anticipate Audience Objections

"To avoid criticism say nothing, do nothing, be nothing." – **Aristotle**

No matter how well-researched and thought out the content of your presentation is, there may be someone in the audience (or multiple attendees) who disagrees with, objects to or wants to challenge your message. And they may or may not wait until the formal Question and Answer session to voice their objection. That's been my experience over the years. As a result, I now anticipate (dare I say, "expect"?) audience objections. I recommend you do the same.

Anticipating audience objections does two things: 1) It allows me to be prepared should the moment arise and I'm able to fairly naturally appear confident and knowledgeable despite the sudden audience objection. I'm not completely caught off guard. Avoiding being caught off guard helps me maintain control in front of the audience. 2) It helps me to remain credible in front of the audience. Let's say an objection arises and I am not at least somewhat prepared to address it. The audience may give me the benefit of the doubt that the audience member surprised me with an objection for which I

37

do not have a handy response. But let's say a second audience member also raises an objection later in the presentation. If again I appear caught off guard and unprepared with at least some thoughtful, knowledgeable response, the credibility of my entire presentation's message may suddenly be at risk. I'm recommending you avoid that risk during your preparation.

Here's what I do to help me anticipate audience objections, challenges and even negative comments specific to the content of my presentation.

- As I write the content of the presentation and insert key points I regularly pause and ask myself, **"What if...?"**

    o "**What if** someone in the audience disagrees with this statement and actually offers conflicting information aloud for all to hear? How will I respond?"

    o "**What if** someone in the audience speaks negatively about a point I have explained saying aloud that the information is useless? How will I respond?"

    o "**What if** someone in the audience wants to know where I obtained the information because they just do not believe what I am saying? How will I respond?"

By regularly asking myself, **"What if...?"** during the creation of my content, I feel as prepared as possible for audience-generated questions, disagreements and negative comments.

After your content is created and you're satisfied with what you've written, it's time to start preparing for presenting your message. *We focus on delivering your message in Section Three of this book.*

Section Three

Presenting Powerfully

SECTION 3, CHAPTER 14

Practice Often

"Before anything else, preparation is the key to success."
– Alexander Graham Bell

I'm a big fan of practicing the presentation in the weeks and days prior to the actual event (speech, video, business meeting, seminar, etc.). The saying goes, "Practice makes perfect." I'm not sure we're ever "perfect," but I am certain that practice increases our confidence. And a confident presenter is a powerful presenter.

The more often I practice, the more I become familiar with the content. The more familiar with the content, the more confident I am. The more confident I am, the more in control and prepared I come across to the audience. From that point, the sky is the limit.

As soon as your presentation content is finalized, start practicing how you will deliver it.

- Practice your opening remarks. Remember, GRAB their attention immediately.

- Practice your transitions between sections. Your goal is to keep everything flowing smoothly.

- Practice your closing.

- Practice, practice, practice.

A bonus benefit of regular practice is you can get a good sense of the strong, so-so and weak elements of your presentation. You'll have opportunities to work through improving your presentation by speaking it aloud during practice without the audience. You'll get a feel for which sections in your presentation need fine-tuning and, possibly, even more practice time.

I like to practice my presentation openings as well as the transitions between sections the most frequently. With regard to the openings, it's been my experience that if I start out solid, my confidence receives an immediate boost that generally lasts the entire presentation. That boost is secured during practice time. Likewise, by rehearsing the transitions between sections I have a sense of control of how the entire presentation will unfold. That sense of control allows me to increase my command of the material and keep the audience focused and engaged.

- Practice your opening when you're driving around running errands.

- Practice your transitions in the house in front of a mirror (or not) when no one is home.

- Practice key sections on a walk (I do it when I go for a run or a bike ride). Don't worry about who sees you talking to yourself!

- Practice in front of a family member or friend if you want some early feedback on how the audience might react.

There is nothing more important, in my experience, than practice and preparation. Nothing. It has served me very well my entire public speaking career. Plus, ***practice helps reduce nervousness, which we discuss next.***

Expect Nerves

"Courage doesn't mean you don't get afraid. Courage means you don't let fear stop you." – **Bethany Hamilton**

No amount of preparation completely eliminates the feeling of nervousness prior to making a presentation. As I write this chapter of the book, I know I have to make a presentation at an important business meeting later in the day. I'm prepared. I've practiced. And I'm still nervous. But it's not a crippling nervousness. It's not going to cause me to freeze when it's my turn to speak (fingers crossed!). Instead, it's what I like to call a "healthy amount" of nerves that keeps me grounded, humble and prevents me from taking the presentation for granted. I'm still going to invest the necessary time to prepare for the creation and delivery of the message no matter how many years I've been presenting so that when it's show time I'm as ready as possible. I'm still going to rehearse my opening remarks and my transitions. But I'll still be a bit nervous.

That's normal. And it's to be expected. In fact, I'll be a bit worried if the day should come when I'm not a little nervous about making a presentation. That may signal I've become too comfortable and possibly overconfident.

Remember this, too: We're nervous because we care. We're nervous because the message to be delivered and our performance are important to us. It's natural to be a little nervous about how the message will be received, about how our delivery of the content will be heard, and about what the audience will most remember after you say goodbye.

Expect nerves every time. Recognize why they arrive. Remember a recent presentation that also made you nervous and how you nevertheless delivered a solid performance. Nerves are normal.

One way I manage my nerves is by arriving early for the presentation; which is what we discuss next.

Arrive Early

"90% of how well the talk will go is determined before the speaker steps on the platform." – **Somers White**

I'm a sports fan so I refer to any speaking engagement or presentation that I'll be delivering as "game day." That's what I call it in my mind. It brings a little fun to the presentation for me. It also heightens the specialness of the day for me. I strongly recommend always arrive early on game day. Arrive as early as is reasonably possible. I generally arrive 2 hours or more prior to the start of any presentation, depending on what "day of" final preparation has to be performed.

Here's the reality for me: I'm already a little nervous about the presentation. I do not want to compound those nerves by running late arriving to the facility or meeting room; then rushing around last-minute conducting any final preparation before the program starts. Before you know it, the audience is filling the seats (or the scheduled video session is about to begin).

Additionally, by arriving early I usually can carve out some final quiet moments to gather my thoughts, take a few deep breaths and calmly take the stage ready to grab the audience's attention (and hold their attention, hopefully!).

Here's my recommended **"game day checklist"** before the presentation:

- Arrive 2 hours early or more.
- Find the meeting room.
- Assess the layout of the meeting room, where you'll be standing, where you'll be positioning any visual aids/props and handouts for easy access (do this even if all of these details were previously arranged and ironed out).
- Test the microphone/sound system (and any other technology).
- Make sure the screen is easily viewed by all audience members.
- Be able to dim the lights in the meeting room as needed.
- Find the restroom.
- Have a bottle of water handy to overcome dry mouth.
- 15 minutes before the start take a short walk alone for final thought gathering, self-pep talk and opening remarks rehearsal.

Your name has been announced. It's time to take the stage. Where will you stand on that stage?

Stand to the Left

*"You don't have to be great to start, but
you do have to start to be great."*
– Zig Ziglar

If I am presenting to an audience with a large projection screen displaying slides and visuals, I try to always stand to the left side of the screen (looking at the screen from the audience's viewpoint). Why? Because people read from left to right. That's the natural flow of our eyes. We start on the left and continue reading the words, graphics and visuals to the right. I want the audience to do the same. It's already automatic for them so I'll position myself in that visual auto zone. Thus, they'll see me first – as the message leader -- and naturally continue on to the right with their eyes to read or see any content on the projection screen.

Sometimes the layout of the room in which I'm presenting does not allow me to stand to the left. So I stand to the right of the screen and make the best of it. It's not the end of the world, but I can see the audience has to work a little harder to both look at me and then shift their eyes back to the screen. It's just not as smooth. And if you take me up on my other recommendations in this book to be animated, use gestures, move around a bit when driving home a point, you'll make it much easier on your audience if all of that movement you make happens on their left side of the projection screen.

You're in position next to the screen. ***The audience is looking at you. Look right back into their eyes; which is our next chapter.***

Make Eye Contact

"To sway an audience, you must watch them as you speak." – **C. Kent Wright**

One of the most powerful public speaking tools presenters have has nothing to do with their voice or their words. It's their eyes. Make eye contact with the audience throughout the duration of the presentation. Literally look into their eyes. Try to work the entire room with your eyes. Look to your left. Look to your right. Include everyone. Your eyes will help keep the audience engaged in your presentation. It will help them feel included and involved.

While you're making eye contact throughout the room you'll likely notice a few extra engaged audience members who may even give you a friendly smile. It will be apparent they are very much interested in your presentation. I try to make eye contact with those folks more frequently to help further fuel me. It's rewarding and motivating when an audience member lets you know, "Hey, what you're presenting is interesting to me!"

Likewise, as you're working the room with your eyes you'll notice some folks who are not engaged. In fact, some in the audience may be doodling, looking at their phone, or talking to the person next to them. You may see faces that clearly express to you they are bored out of their mind. Unfortunately, you may even see someone falling asleep. I have. It's OK. It happens and what I've learned to do is to focus on the remainder of the audience in the room. I'll seek those extra engaged faces to reassure me the presentation is still going smoothly.

And that's another reason to always work the entire room with your eyes. It's a way for you to measure your message's impact and your delivery style's effectiveness. If you're noticing dozens of audience members losing interest, it's time to reevaluate the presentation: the content or your delivery style or both. But a person or two not engaged is to be expected.

When you arrive early to assess the room and where you'll be standing during the presentation, be sure it's a location from which you can fairly easily see the entire room. And then make eye contact start to finish.

Another powerful presenter's tool is gesturing. That's our next chapter.

SECTION 3, CHAPTER 19

Use Hand Gestures

"Act as if what you do makes a difference."
– Auguste Rodin

Strategically timed hand and arm gestures can be powerful elements of a presenter's toolbox. They can help you make a particular point in your speech or highlight a key section in your video. An animated presenter is an attention-grabbing presenter. And that's what you want, the audience's attention. An energetic and excited presenter cannot help but be noticed by the audience. Allow your energy to funnel through your gestures. But don't force them. They need to come across to the viewer in a natural way. They should not be excessive, either. Through practice (see "Practice Often" on page 41), and watching yourself in videos (see "Video Yourself" on page 91), you'll get a good sense of the appropriate amount of gesturing for your presentation.

Here are a few examples of gestures that have worked very well for me:

- ***Finger point.*** If I'm making a key statement by declaring "That's what *you* want..." I'll finish the statement with a direct finger point at an audience member and look straight into his or her eyes.

- ***Shoulder shrug.*** If I'm raising an important question for the audience to consider, I'll shrug my shoulders just as I'm ending the question.

- ***Arm movements.*** Freely moving my arms up and down and to the sides as I present adds power to my spoken words.

In addition to gestures, I also recommend taking strategic steps toward the audience to bring emphasis to certain parts of your presentation. Literally walk a little closer to the audience (if your meeting room allows such movement). A few steps toward the audience can really capture their attention.

Practice gestures and movement at home in private. Do it in front of the mirror. As you incorporate them into your presentation try to read your audience's reaction. You'll get a feel for how well it's working. Then watch yourself in a video to self-evaluate. Adjust your animation as needed. Soon, gestures and taking steps during the presentation will feel automatic and natural.

Physical movement by the presenter enhances the delivered message. So does silence. We discuss that next.

SECTION 3, CHAPTER 20

Pause...to Pull Them In

"The most precious things in speech are the...pauses." – **Sir Ralph Richardson**

I like to insert a deliberate pause of a few seconds into my presentations in special locations to emphasize a point, to bring attention to a thought, or to highlight that we're about to transition into a new section. Done appropriately and without excess, pauses can pull your audience in even further than they already were. There's something powerful about a few extra seconds of silence that captures the listening audience. "Why is he pausing? What's he about to say next? The room just got quiet. Why?"

During your practice sessions alone you can experiment with inserting pauses into your presentation. And then you can evaluate if you have inserted them appropriately when you unleash the pauses during actual presentations you are delivering. As you look into your audiences' eyes, you'll see whether they are following your words closely or not. A well-timed pause can help keep the audience very much in the moment. Take advantage of pauses.

Use volume to your advantage, too. We discuss that next.

Vary Your Volume

*"Speech is power: Speech is to persuade,
to convert, to compel."*
– Ralph Waldo Emerson

The best written speech, video script or presentation is useless if the audience cannot hear it. I'm not going to spend much time on the importance of speaking loud enough to be heard other than to say this: speak loud enough for everyone in the audience to easily hear you; and if it's necessary to use a microphone, use one. I prefer a wireless, clip-on microphone that attaches to my shirt near my neck to keep my hands free for gesturing and picking up any props or visual aids I may use.

It's also important to vary your volume during the presentation. Intentionally speaking a little lower than normal or purposely raising your voice can further grab your audience's attention during moments you feel are extra important. Is there a theme you're really trying to drive home? Is there a bottom line message you're finally revealing? Consider varying your volume. Not only does changing your volume draw increased attention to your spoken words, it automatically makes what you're saying more interesting because it's different – it's being said quieter or louder.

Just like gestures, however, do not vary your volume in excess. That will wear out your audience. Find a nice blend of occurrences. You'll know how often to do it by practicing it in private (see "Practice Often" on page 41) and then testing it in real time with actual audiences. As you look into their eyes making contact, evaluate the effectiveness of your varied volume. Did it work? Did their faces light up with increased interest? If not, adjust next time.

An adjustment I have had to make during presentations pertains to speed. That's our next topic.

Slow Down

"It does not matter how slowly you go, so long as you do not stop." – **Confucius**

I tend to have a lot of natural energy. On top of that, I'm generally very excited for my speaking engagements with a touch of nervousness. You add all of that up: natural energy + excited + nerves and it's a recipe for a *fast-talking* presenter. Talking quickly usually makes it difficult on the audience to fully follow the message. I have to remind myself to speak at an appropriate pace for the benefit of the audience trying to listen. Early in my career I often received constructive criticism from the audience: "Slow down. You're speaking too quickly. It's hard to keep up with you when you speak that fast."

There will be times within a presentation I intentionally pick up the pace of my talk to emphasize a point or to draw extra attention to a theme, but overall I try to be mindful of my speed. I don't want to be too slow (Too slow risks putting the audience to sleep). And I don't want to be too fast (Too fast risks losing the audience). I try to find a happy medium with a slight lean toward semi-fast.

Someone gave me a tip years ago to help me be mindful to slow down during a presentation: stop to **drink water**. I position a glass of water near where I stand for a presentation. I force myself every 15 minutes or so to stop and take a sip of water. Often I very much need the sip to keep my mouth from getting too dry. But many times my mouth is just fine but the pause to drink forces a hard break in the presentation that helps to keep the pace manageable for the audience.

During your practice time (see "Practice Often" on page 41) after you have become comfortable with the content of your presentation, spend some time focused on your speed of delivery. Ask yourself, "Was that too fast, too slow or just about right?" Rehearse in front of a family member or friend for their pace feedback. And watch yourself in a video (see "Video Yourself" on page 91). That will help you determine if your pace is appropriate for your listening audience.

Your audience will let you know if you're speaking too quickly if you ask them for feedback. We'll talk more about collecting formal feedback from the audience in "Collect and USE the Audience's Feedback" on page 97).

Now it's time to enhance the presentation with visuals. That's the next chapter.

SECTION 3, CHAPTER 23

Use Visual Aids

"Quality is not an act. It's a habit."
– Aristotle

A well-written and delivered presentation (or video or seminar) can be enhanced with the use of visual aids or props. I'm not talking about the use of a slideshow (but I do discuss creating and using slides in "Use a Slideshow to Enhance Your Presentation" on page 34). Here I am referring to physical props that show the audience what it is you're describing (for example, running shoes, energy gels and apparel if I were doing a presentation about **"Running Can Change Your Life for the Better: Here's How and How to Get Started."**). Having visual aids for the audience to see in person (or captured on camera in your video) helps them further understand the message you're communicating. They can provide a complimentary learning point to accompany your spoken words. Here are tips for using props that have worked very well for me in my public speaking career.

- **Keep the props nearby.** Make sure all props are within a few steps from where you are presenting. You don't want to be scrambling searching for your props when it's time to show them. It makes you look unprepared. I like to have a table just a few feet behind me and off to the side completely reserved for my props.

- **Hold the prop so that everyone can see it.** If I'm going to go to the trouble to show a prop, I'm going to make certain I hold it high enough and long enough for everyone in the room to see. Otherwise, why am I even using the prop? With the prop high in my hands above my head I like to take a few steps to my right, a few steps to my left, and few steps forward from the center position so that everyone in the audience can see it. And rarely do I worry that I'm spending too much time with the prop in my hands because I usually continue to present (talk) while holding the prop. It is sometimes frustrating for the audience knowing the presenter is holding a prop, but they cannot see it very well because the presenter is not holding it high enough, long enough, and is not moving a little closer for their vantage point. Work to avoid that audience frustration.

- **Do not pass the props around the room.** You might be thinking, "Why not just pass the prop around the room after briefly holding it high so that everyone in the audience for sure has an opportunity to see it up close?" I strongly recommend against that. I have done that, and it did not go well. As soon as you pass a prop around the room the attention switches completely to the prop; and anything you might be saying while it is passed around is no longer the focal point. As the presenter, your spoken words combined with any props IN YOUR HANDS must always be the focal point. Do not disconnect them. Try this instead: Tell the audience that they are welcome to look at the entire table of props at the end of the presentation. Even if an audience member asks, "Can I please see that up close?" politely say, "I invite everyone to take a closer look at all of the props behind me on the table after the presentation, but I please want to continue."

Another important "do not" we should discuss next is the temptation to read your slideshow aloud.

SECTION 3, CHAPTER 24

Do Not Read Your Slideshow to the Audience

"Self-trust is the first secret of success."
– Ralph Waldo Emerson

No matter how well I think I can read aloud and make what I'm reading sound interesting and exciting, if all I'm bringing to the party is a well-read slideshow I have shortchanged my audience. The audience can read the slides themselves. If I'm reading word-for-word the exact content of the slides, the audience does not need me. The audience will quickly realize that the "presentation" is a reading of the words on the screen. They'll start to lose interest and focus. They may even exit. Why? They didn't come to be read to. They came to participate in an engaging, well-thought-out and delivered presentation.

I have been in the audience of a presentation in which the speaker read the slides for 90% of the presentation. Out of respect for a fellow presenter, I stayed for the duration. However, I could not wait for it to end.

Here's my rule of thumb to keep me from becoming a reader: I force myself to reveal only a fraction of the actual presentation in the slideshow. Knowing that, I won't be tempted to just read the slides because doing so is only giving the audience a portion of the presentation. They deserve the full presentation. The full presentation is much more than the slideshow. The slideshow is only a detailed index of topics and talking points. Behind those topics and talking points are the additional facts, stories, statistics, examples, case studies, research results, etc. that are not on the screen. And if they are on the screen, they're only "teased." The full story about those topics and talking points comes from the presenter's mind.

Let me expand on this. If an audience member was given my slideshow word-for-word he or she would only be in possession of about 33% of my actual presentation. Because the remaining 67% is revealed "live" during the presentation from my mind. It's not on the screen. Thus, I'm not going to bother reading what's on the screen to the audience knowing it's only 1/3 of the presentation.

Don't be a reader. Be a presenter.

Now it's time to get the audience involved in the presentation. We discuss that next.

SECTION 3, CHAPTER 25

Get the Audience Involved

"Tell me and I forget. Teach me and I remember. Involve me and I learn."
– Benjamin Franklin

Getting the audience involved helps to further engage them in your presentation. It injects an extra element of interest beyond your spoken words and any visuals you might be showing. It helps to keep them from getting bored.

A successful way I have involved my audiences over the years is by asking a question aloud to kick off the next key topic or section. Allow an audience member to provide the answer. If the answer is wrong, thank the person and seek the next audience member's answer. If after the third attempted answer no one in the audience has properly provided the correct answer, I recommend you say the answer aloud and thank everyone for participating.

If possible, raise the stakes a bit by giving a small gift or premium as a "thank you" to anyone who participates. There are many businesses that make fun premiums that can feature your company logo which will reinforce your brand long after your presentation has ended (apparel, office needs, outdoor activities, etc.). Once the audience realizes you are giving away gifts in exchange for their participation, you might see a spike in their involvement. Have fun with it!

A word of caution: Space your audience participation moments strategically throughout your presentation. Be mindful to not do it too frequently or else it may lose its effectiveness or worse it could become a burden on your audience – regardless how cool your giveaway item is. I suggest 2 to 3 (max) audience participation moments for every hour of your presentation (that's 1 every 20 minutes), but by all means test and evaluate this for yourself in your presentations. You'll get a sense pretty quickly if you're doing it too frequently. How will you know?

- Very few audience members are willing to participate.
- Their facial expressions say, "Not again."
- It feels forced to you.

If done in the proper doses, I'm confident that purposely involving your audience will enhance the overall experience of your presentation for them and for you.

Asking rhetorical questions is another way to engage and involve the audience. Let's look at that next.

Ask the Audience Rhetorical Questions

"Success is walking from failure to failure
with no loss of enthusiasm."
– Winston Churchill

I have found that asking the audience rhetorical questions (questions for which you really do not want them to answer; at least not out loud) at key moments is an effective way to transition to an extra important topic or to bring heightened emphasis to a special part of the presentation.

Earlier we identified a possible presentation topic **"Running Can Change Your Life for the Better: Here's How and How to Get Started"** (page 19). Here are sample rhetorical questions I might insert into that presentation:

- *"Why 4 weeks? Why can't I just commit to it for 2 weeks to see if running is for me?"* (An example rhetorical question to help explain why it's critical to stick with a new running program for at least one month before entertaining thoughts of quitting. Two weeks is not sufficient time and here's why.)

- ***"Who says running improves my health?"*** (An attention-grabbing pointed rhetorical question that some in the audience very well may be thinking. You boldly brought it to the forefront and now you're going to answer it.)

You'll have to pick your moments and sprinkle in the rhetorical questions only a handful of times to avoid it becoming too expected and overused. Experiment during your practice time (see "Practice Often" on page 41). Implement it during actual presentations and self-evaluate how well it went.

Be prepared for the engaged audience member who takes your rhetorical question seriously and wants to offer an answer by either raising his or her hand or saying the answer aloud for all to hear.

- If a hand suddenly rises in the audience I recommend you politely look that audience member in the eyes and thank the person <u>but continue on presenting without seeking his or her answer</u>. "That was a rhetorical question, but thank you."

- If the audience member speaks aloud without being called upon, I recommend you say:

  o "Yes, that's right. Thank you," and keep presenting from there (If the audience member said the answer you wanted.)

  o "Thank you. Actually the answer is ..." and supply the correct answer for everyone to hear and keep presenting from there. (There's more information about this topic in "Keep Control of the Room and the Audience" on page 81).

This will become second nature to you as you practice it during rehearsals and for sure as you implement it into your presentations. It's become a very effective tool for me.

A Question and Answer session with the audience is another useful tool you can use. We'll discuss that next.

Allow Time for a Formal Q & A Session

"Success does not come to you...
you go to it." – **Marva Collins**

There's a lot of value in including a formal Question and Answer session in your presentation if your format allows it.

- It helps the audience feel involved (which enhances their overall experience).

- It could spark a new content idea for your future presentations (or a video you might produce, or an industry article you might write).

- It provides an opportunity to clarify any information that the audience possibly did not fully grasp earlier (which also gives you a chance to evaluate if your coverage of that content could/should be improved or modified).

- It opens the door for useful information exchange "live" on the spot among the audience. (And if that happens, you'll be remembered as the presenter who afforded that opportunity).

Here are my tips for a smooth and successful Q & A.

A) <u>Wait until you are finished with your presentation before opening the floor to a formal Q & A.</u> Doing so will prevent an audience member(s) from derailing your presentation. Explain during the introduction of your presentation that there will be ample time at the end for questions and that you will be waiting until that time to entertain any questions. NOTE: Such a message during the introduction will not prevent audience members from still raising their hand during the presentation. For those situations, I offer you my next tip...

B) <u>You do not have to take a question just because a hand rises in the audience.</u> For any hand that rises during the presentation that you know you will not be addressing immediately, quickly look that audience member in the eye (all the while still presenting) and show him or her your index finger indicating "Wait a minute, please." And keep presenting. Do not stop. And do not circle back to that audience member until the formal Q & A. It's been my experience that person will realize all questions will be asked and answered at the very end. And should that attendee's hand rise again, just briefly say aloud mid-presentation, "I'm going to take all questions during the formal Q & A at the very end so we can stay on track with the presentation." Audiences have told me they understand and respect this approach.

C) <u>Don't let any attendee dominate the Q & A.</u> Be on the watch for the attendee who wants to dominate with either a very long-winded question or story and/or wants to ask so many questions very few other attendees have time to ask their questions. Here's my strategy for these two delicate situations without being rude.

- o **(For the long-winded question)** Earnestly looking for a break-point in the attendee's long question I'll inject, "Could you summarize your question briefly for us?" or "So, you're basically asking ..." (and then I do my own shortened version of the question).

- o **(For the long-winded story)** This is tricky territory. You do not want to be rude, but you also cannot afford to let one person drain minutes and minutes of the presentation. After a reasonable amount of time has elapsed I will say to the attendee, "That is a really interesting situation you are explaining. I'd like to hear more about it after the presentation please. Let's keep things moving with our next question please."

- ○ **(For the attendee asking so many questions few others get a chance)** If the same person keeps raising his or her hand to ask questions during the formal Q & A, be sure to allow other attendees to also ask questions. Make a point to pick other people before circling back to the same attendee for his or her 2nd, 3rd or 4th question. Even if no one else is raising his or her hand to ask a question and you only have one attendee participating, I'll say aloud, "I want to give others a chance to ask a question before I go back to the same person. Does anyone else have a question?" If no one does, you can return to the original attendee with the knowledge you gave others a chance.

BONUS Presenting TIP:

If the formal Question & Answer Session is going rather quietly – meaning few attendees are asking questions or perhaps no one has a question – you could offer your own questions and answers from your past presentations. Share out loud a question or two previous attendees asked. Reveal the answer. Do this once or twice and it just might trigger audience members to start asking their own questions.

Fielding questions within a presentation is a skill that will improve over time through repetition. ***Being willing to tell the audience, "I do not know" also improves with time. That's our next topic.***

Tell the Audience, "I Don't Know"

"Only those who dare to fail greatly
can ever achieve greatly."
– Robert F. Kennedy

Even if your presentation does not set aside time for a formal
Question & Answer session, it's very possible an audience
member will raise his or her hand and want to ask a question. Don't fake an answer if you do not know the actual
answer to the question. If you think you can cleverly make up
an answer to get you out of the moment and close the books
on that person's question without knowing the real answer,
avoid that temptation. Do not feel compelled that as the presenter you must know the answer to every question that may
surface. That's not only unrealistic; you could dig yourself
into an uncomfortable hole in front of everyone. You risk
being called to task by someone in the audience who has
accurate information specific to the question and now you're
going to have to explain the conflicting information you offered aloud. Instead, I recommend honestly saying, "I do not
know the answer to that. Let me please look into it and I'll
get back to you." Then follow-up by obtaining a way to send a
response to the audience member (for example, an email).

What I have found to be a successful way to address questions for which I do not know the answer is to ask the audience at large to help. "That's a great question. And I do not know the answer. Does anyone in the room know the answer?" And then see if someone is willing to offer information aloud. If no one does, I fall back on my offer, "Let me please look into that and I'll get back to you."

It's a comfortable and confident presenter who is willing to admit not knowing the answer and then ask the audience for help. ***Be careful to maintain control of the room, however. We discuss that next.***

Keep Control of the Room (and the Audience)

"Challenges are what make life interesting and overcoming them is what makes life meaningful." – **Joshua Marine**

Inevitably during the course of your public speaking career you'll encounter disruptive attendees. I have found these are people who are not fully engaged, their focus on the content is lacking, and no amount of your passion will change that. I have experienced disruptive attendees many times. I used to handle them poorly. I now handle them better. Here are my suggestions for successfully dealing with the two most common types of attendee-generated disruptions I have faced.

- ***Ringing Cell Phones.*** I make a point during the introduction of the presentation to announce "housekeeping items." These notes include where the attendees can find the restrooms, a reminder that handouts/resources will be offered at the end of the program so attendees don't have to take detailed notes if they don't want to (see "Save Handouts Until the End" on page 94), and a mention that I'd like each attendee to fill out a feedback form before they leave (see "Collect and USE the Audience's Feedback" on page 97). And then I talk about cell phones.

> *"So that everyone in the room can focus on the presentation and minimize distractions, would you kindly silence your cell phones? If you absolutely have to take an important phone call, please leave the room quickly to take the call. On behalf of everyone in the room, thank you for cooperating."*

Once I started making that cell phone announcement it eliminated 90% of the cell phone interruptions. Here's what I recommend you do for the other 10% of the time. If a cell phone rings during your presentation, pause a few extra seconds to allow the ring to be heard by everyone. Your silence draws extra attention to the ring. That usually is enough motivation for the offending attendee to quickly silence the phone. If that does not work, your silence will give time for the neighboring attendees to give a "look" at the offending attendee. If that does not work, keep presenting and ignore the disruption.

- ***Attendees talking non-stop to each other.*** This is personally difficult because I put so much thought and energy into the creation and delivery of each presentation that I am surprised attendees would rather chat with each other throughout the presentation than listen, engage and participate. It happens. My first strategy to stop the chatter involves physically moving a little closer to where the talking attendees are in the room. Sometimes hearing and seeing the presenter getting physically closer to their location puts an end to their side conversations. If that does not work, I'll take strategic pauses of a few seconds so that my silence highlights their disruption for everyone to hear. Neighboring attendees may give them a "look." They may become a bit self-conscious and finally stop the chatter. If neither of these approaches works, I recommend you continue with your presentation ignoring the disruption as best you can. Focus on everyone else in the room who is respectfully paying attention.

Here's another less "hostile" disruption that comes from engaged attendees that I would like to alert you about and how I handle it.

- ***Random comments said aloud.*** There may be attendees listening intently to your presentation and following along carefully and then suddenly out loud they'll blurt comments such as "Really?" or "Wow" or "I don't believe that. Are you sure?" These attendees are not raising their hands to ask a question or make a statement. They don't wait to be called upon by the presenter. They just speak out loud while you are presenting. Depending on what is said I will either smile and point to the attendee (sort of acknowledging I heard the comment) or I will briefly say, "We can talk more about it during the Q & A at the end" (which is my polite way of shutting it down until it's time for mass audience commentary).

Keeping control of the room while simultaneously staying focused on delivering your presentation is a juggling skill that you'll improve with experience. Do not become discouraged.

Speaking of discouragement, don't let a modest turnout for your presentation bring you down either. We discuss that next.

84

Deliver Your Best Regardless
of Audience Turnout

*"To give anything less than your best
is to sacrifice your gift."*
– Steve Prefontaine

I have no trouble getting pumped up to make a presentation for a large crowd. There's something about a packed house that just adds to the buzz in the room and the excitement of the moment. As far as I'm concerned, the larger the crowd the better. But what if the number of the people in the audience is only a few? Truthfully, it's one of the biggest challenges I continue to battle in my public speaking career. It is significantly harder for me to get excited to speak in front of a small crowd compared to a large crowd. It just doesn't feel as special to me. That's a mindset I'm recommending you avoid. Every speaking engagement for every audience is special. I have to remind myself of that continuously.

Very early in my career, a colleague traveling with me during a week of presentations in various cities pulled me aside afterward asking, "Paul, what happened out there today? You were not nearly as energetic and passionate as you were yesterday. Why?" When I explained that yesterday's crowd of 100 attendees extra energized me but today's crowd of 10 was a bit of a letdown he said, "Those 10 people today attended and deserved your best just like yesterday's 100. You have to put the crowd size aside mentally." I have never forgotten that advice.

Here are two tips that have helped me get motivated to present to a small crowd that might help you if you also need motivation:

- With about 15 minutes to go before the start of the presentation, I find a quiet place and remind myself that today's audience deserves my absolute best. They came to listen and learn. I'm not going to let them down.

- I pretend someone special in my life (my wife, my daughter, my mom) is in the crowd and I want to showcase my presentation skills.

Make a strong effort to stay pumped up for each speaking engagement regardless of the number of people in the room.

Staying pumped up is much easier if you are well-rested. That's our next topic.

SECTION 3, CHAPTER 31

Stay Rested and Prepared

"The greatest danger for most of us is not that our aim is too high and we miss it, but that it is too low and we reach it."
– Michelangelo

I feel an obligation to the audience to be prepared for the speaking engagement every time. The attendees have taken time out of their days to show up for the presentation. I owe it to them to be ready. That means getting the necessary rest leading up to the presentation, investing the necessary practice and prep time prior to the presentation, and mentally wrapping my mind around, "Today is Game Day."

I've been presenting since 1998. It might be understandable if I were to allow a speaking engagement here or there to receive a little less than my "A" preparation effort or if I stayed out late the night before. After all – I might tell myself – it's the 4th consecutive presentation day in the week smack in the middle of a continuous 12-week "tour" of presentations. What's wrong with "winging it" for 1 or 2 presentations and celebrating a little late at night? I will not allow that to happen out of respect for the audience and respect for our profession.

Here are my recommendations to maintain a high level of rest and preparation.

1. <u>Go to bed early</u> enough to feel well rested. Always. There will be time for late nights but not the eve of a presentation.

2. <u>Wake up early</u> enough to allow time to calmly go through your "game day" routine. This is not the day to be running late and rushing around.

3. <u>Eat</u> something before you take the stage so that you're not overly hungry. You're about to be in the spotlight working hard for the audience. Take in some fuel (a banana, a bagel, something).

4. <u>Exercise</u> (a walk, a run, a bike ride, a gym session, etc.) to help you relieve any built-up stress, clear your mind and stay healthy.

5. <u>Never stop practicing</u> your openings, transitions and your overall presentation. Just when you think to yourself, "I don't need to practice today because I've got it," you slip, get sloppy and lose your edge.

You'll appreciate your commitment to being rested and prepared when you ***watch yourself on video one day. That's our next topic.***

SECTION 3, CHAPTER 32

Video Yourself

*"It's what you practice in private that you
will be rewarded for in public."*
– Tony Robbins

I recommend every few years making a video of yourself; a video that captures you on screen delivering your speech or presentation. This is a valuable self-assessment and self-improvement tool. While I like to think that I have a good sense of my presentation style and abilities and which areas may need fine-tuning and improvement, nothing is more revealing than actually seeing myself in a video. Seeing is believing.

Hire someone to video your presentation and then watch the video with the following in mind:

- **How is my pace?** Am I too fast, too slow, or just about right?

- **How is my volume?** Can I be heard easily? And am I adjusting my volume for emphasis at the appropriate times during the presentation? Am I too loud?

- **How do I sound?** Am I speaking clearly or am I slurring my words?

- **How is my eye contact with the audience?** Am I giving everyone in the room quality eye time?

- **How is my body language?** Are my gestures appropriate for the talking points I am making?

- **How am I positioned?** Are the visual aids, props and handouts too far away to easily access?

- **How is my spacing?** Am I too close, too far away or just right in relationship to the audience? Do I move closer to the audience at strategic moments to drive home a point?

- **How does the slideshow look?** Can the audience clearly see what's on screen?

I have hired a video company for many years, and it's allowed me to objectively assess my performances. I am confident you'll find it to be a beneficial self-improvement tool.

Additionally, depending on how you market and promote your presentation to your target audience, you could extract video clips to promote your presentation as part of your overall marketing and advertising campaign.

A quick glance at your wristwatch (I wear one to keep track of my timing) shows you're just about to wrap up today's presentation. ***There's just a few more business matters to tackle that you purposely held for the end. We discuss those next.***

Save Handouts Until the End

*"Do what you can with all you
have wherever you are."*
– Theodore Roosevelt

I'm a big fan of offering the audience a handout. Capturing key principles from your presentation in a formal written handout(s) (a single sheet, a booklet or multiple pamphlets), is a great way to help summarize the content of the presentation and provide the audience with reference material for the future. The best time to distribute the handouts is <u>at the very end of the presentation</u>. Not in the beginning. Not in the middle. Hold all handouts until the very end. Here's why.

I believe handouts are meant to supplement the presentation and assist with understanding the content ***after the presentation is over.*** They are reference materials for the future. If you distribute the reference materials at any point during the presentation before the end, you risk the audience focusing on the handout and not paying attention to you, the presenter, and anything you will be saying or showing.

- You do not want your audience reading handouts while you're delivering the presentation. They'll miss the information you're describing <u>aloud</u> that is not in the handouts (stories, examples, case studies, etc.).

- You do not want your audience thumbing through handouts while you're showing your slideshow (see "Use a Slideshow to Enhance Your Presentation" on page 34). They'll miss out on key visuals <u>on the screen</u> that are not featured in the handouts (graphs, statistics, photographs, etc.).

- You don't want the handouts to be a source of side conversations among attendees distracting from the primary topic of the moment.

- And before you ask, "Why not just include *everything* from the presentation in the handouts, distribute them at the start, and let the audience follow along word-for-word, picture-for-picture during the presentation?" That's not a handout. That's a book. And the audience certainly does not need me for them to read a book.

Another important reason to delay handout distribution until the end of the presentation is it allows you to control the unveiling of information. You decide when a topic is revealed. You determine the sequence of key points. That's your specialty. You're a professional presenter. If the audience has a handout during the presentation and chooses to look ahead at an upcoming topic, someone may be tempted to ask a question about it right now. And while you're well equipped to handle such questions, it's an avoidable detour – avoidable if you save handouts until the very end.

Over the years I have experimented with the best time to distribute handouts. I have witnessed the results of handout distribution at various points of time during my presentations. The end of the presentation is the best time. It allows the audience to fully pay attention to the presentation content and then exit armed with useful resources for their future reference.

But don't let them exit just yet. There's one final thing we need from the audience...

Collect and USE the Audience's Feedback

"Experience is the teacher of all things."
– Julius Caesar

The best person to evaluate the usefulness of your presentation topic as well as the effectiveness of your presentation delivery style is the audience member. With all due respect to your family, your colleagues, and any managers that you may report to, none of them is as uniquely qualified to evaluate the value and strength of your content and your presentation skills as the actual audience. If we're honest with ourselves, this makes perfect sense because the presentation (or video, speech, seminar, etc.) is intended for the people in the audience. Talk to your audience.

Deliberately collect feedback from your audience and then use the collected information. You should incorporate what the audience is telling you into your content and into your delivery. It will help you learn and improve. It has for me my entire public speaking career.

What to ask your audience in the questionnaire:

- What did you find most helpful today?

- What was most interesting to you?

- What was not included in the content you wish would be in the future?

- What was your least favorite part?

- Was the program too long, too short or just about right?

- If you had your choice, what time of day would the program happen? What time of year?

- Any other feedback you'd like to provide?

BONUS Feedback Usage TIP:

Audience responses to "What did you find most helpful today?" as well as "What was most interesting to you?" can provide you with testimonials you can use to promote your next presentation via invitations you might mail, E-blasts, Social Media, the internet, etc. Be sure to secure the audience member's permission. I have been fortunate to use audience-supplied testimonials generated specifically from the questionnaire responses. Additionally, audience feedback could spark an idea for industry articles you could author. I've been able to do that successfully over the years.

When to ask your audience for feedback:

- Near the very end of the program. Why? So they can experience the entire program before offering comments. You want their observations about the entire presentation, not just portions of it.

- Always "live" in-person while they are still in the room. Why? Because if you try to do it after they leave, not only is it possible their observations will become fuzzy as time passes, but the likelihood of them actually participating in the feedback process drops significantly. That's been my experience. Get them while the iron is hot if you want candid, top-of-mind feedback, and a high percentage of participation.

How to ask your audience for feedback:

- Use a formal survey questionnaire they'll fill out with a ball point pen. Consider using a carbon copy form to make it easy to produce duplicate copies of the survey results (one copy for your reference and another copy for anyone in your organization that'll need the information or a database management company that you hire to track results).

- Limit the survey form to one side of the sheet. You don't want to overwhelm the audience with a laundry list of questions.

- If you can obtain the desired audience feedback digitally (instead of paper) while they are still "live" in the room, go for it.

Collecting Feedback Tips:

- Give the audience incentive to complete the feedback questionnaire by clearly explaining how important their comments are. Tell them that their input will help improve the program for future audiences. Point out a quick content segment that was added to today's presentation specifically because of past audiences. It'll add credibility that you really do value and use the audience feedback. (**NOTE:** That's a good thing to point out during your presentation, too. Just spend a few seconds saying, "This next topic was requested by past audiences." At the end of the program when you are seeking audience feedback they may remember that you used past audience feedback to create today's presentation. It's a nice reinforcement of the audience-presenter connection.)

- You might also consider teasing the availability of your handouts (pamphlets, brochures, etc.) as motivation for the audience to provide feedback. "In exchange for your completed survey forms, I'll be in the back of the room passing out the booklet that summarizes today's key points from the presentation."

Good luck as you maximize the quantity and quality of audience feedback.

I have one final tip to offer.

SECTION 3, CHAPTER 35

Do it Your Way

"Let's do this." – **Paul Benedict Scelsi**

In my public speaking career, the success – or failure – of any presentation (or video, speech, seminar, etc.) that I delivered to an audience was largely on my shoulders. Yes, I had help. But that help was in a supportive role. The ultimate responsibility of the program was mine. If things went well, the eyes looked at me. If things went so-so, the eyes looked at me. And if things absolutely tanked, the eyes looked at me.

I recommend you write and deliver your presentations – and carry out everything in between (practice, preparation, game day routines) – the way YOU want. No one has more at stake; no one has more on the line; no one will be held more accountable than you. So take ownership and own your stage.

Final Tips:

- If you want to arrive 3 hours early before your presentation, do it. If you prefer only an hour of pre-game preparation, do it.

- If you want the room arranged in a certain way to maximize your comfort in the room and enhance the audience's viewing and listening experience, do it.

- If you want to rehearse your presentation start to finish every day, do it. If instead you only want to practice your opening comments and transitions, do it.

- If you want visual aids or props to help explain a topic, use them.

- Whatever makes you the most dynamic, memorable, easy-to-understand presenter leading your audience to action...do it.

I hope this book has helped you. It's been a joy to write. Happy presenting!

Appendix

Behind the Curtain

Checklist for creating & delivering powerful presentations

☐ Put Yourself in YOUR Audience

☐ Grab their Attention Immediately

☐ Hold their Attention Throughout

☐ Keep it Conversational

☐ Use Transitions to Maintain Flow and Engagement

☐ Combine Content and Passion

☐ Identify the Primary Purpose

☐ List the Supporting Topics

☐ Enhance the Content

☐ Collect More Notes than You'll Use

☐ Read to Stay Current and Creative

☐ Use a Slideshow to Enhance Your Presentation

☐ Anticipate Audience Objections

☐ Practice Often

☐ Expect Nerves

☐ Arrive Early

☐ Stand to the Left

☐ Make Eye Contact

☐ Use Hand Gestures

☐ Pause...to Pull Them In

☐ Vary Your Volume

☐ Slow Down

☐ Use Visual Aids

☐ Do Not Read Your Slideshow to the Audience

☐ Get the Audience Involved

☐ Ask the Audience Rhetorical Questions

☐ Allow Time for a Formal Q & A Session

☐ Tell the Audience, "I Don't Know"

☐ Keep Control of the Room (and the Audience)

☐ Deliver Your Best Regardless of Audience Turnout

☐ Stay Rested and Prepared

☐ Video Yourself

☐ Save Handouts Until the End

☐ Collect and USE the Audience's Feedback

Made in the USA
Monee, IL
13 April 2022

94681800R00066